TRUST AND BETRAYAL
A CHALLENGE OF CHOICE

Saint Germain

Spirit Sourced - Human Made
Through Lah Rahm Ananda
aka Gordon Corwin II

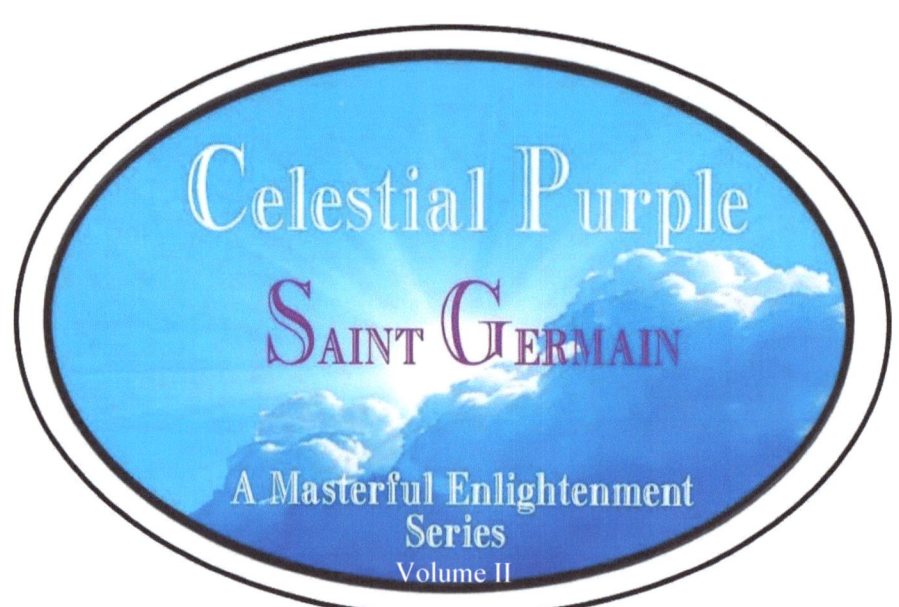

Copyright 2023

ALL RIGHTS RESERVED
INCLUDING THE RIGHT OF REPRODUCTION
IN WHOLE OR IN PART IN ANY FORM

HIGHLAND LIGHT PUBLISHERS IS
A REGISTERED TRADEMARK WITH THE U. S. PATENT
AND TRADEMARK OFFICE. GORDON W. CORWIN II

SPIRIT SOURCED * HUMAN MADE
AI FREE

Saint Germain

Portrait Charles Sindelar

Books by This Author

৵৶

THE SAINT GERMAIN CHRONICLES COLLECTION
A Journey Into Practical Spirituality

VICTORY FOR THE SOUL
Relationships That Work

RISING ABOVE
A Journey To Higher Dimensions

TRUE COMPASSION
Merging Love Into Oneness

DUALITY
In Perspective

TRUST and BETRAYAL
Waters of Truth

GORDON CORWIN II aka LAH RAHN ANANDA on AMAZON Books
Coming soon ... www.SaintGermainBooks.com

OVERVIEW

Among primary building blocks of lasting and Loving Human interactions rests the *keystone of Trust.* With this element anchored in place, honorably supported by integrity and honesty, Earth civilizations have been known to prosper and evolve, collectively and for individuals as well. Tied in closely comes the power of a promise kept beyond any doubt or temptation to wander. Twin Flames and Soul Mates are especially tested to process lessons of Trust, as I include within.

This highly motivational and supportive piece *exposes healing milestones for Mastery* in developing a supreme, visceral way of Being that holds agreements and promises as sacred, starting with yourself. I AM speaking of concrete commitments unto yourself and others, as a matter of unshakeable principle, ... sacred promises from you to you to *honor your agreements, to earn respect, and to BE Trustworthy* in all Relationships. Along this pathway lie hurdles of Broken agreements, Betrayals through lying, Wound Reactivation, Over-testing Boundaries, Calculated Betrayals, Repeaters, Ego blocks to Love and Forgiveness, and Resistance to healing Reconciliations of Love. Honor yourself with Trustworthiness and *crack this nutshell* !

Dare to venture with Me into this Domain of Wisdom, opening doors to complete and Master Trust and Betrayal Healings with Forgiveness, Love, and Surrender ... and to inset the star of Trustworthiness atop the Crown of your Aura.

Gordon Corwin II

With My Love Always,

𝔖aint 𝔊ermain

Through **Lah Rahn Ananda**

TABLE OF CONTENTS

BOOKS BY THIS AUTHOR	INTRO
OVERVIEW	INTRO
THE SAINT GERMAIN TOOLBOX	INTRO
TWIN FLAMES AND SOULMATES	1
TOP CHALLENGES OF CHOICE	3
UNHEALED WOUNDS	5
REMAINING FOCUSED AND JOY	7
PERCEPTIONS OF BETRAYAL	9
PERSONAL HONOR CODE	11
PROCESSING BREACHES OF TRUST	13
ROOTS OF BETRAYAL	15
BOUNDARIES	15
FORGIVENESS AND MASTERY	19
HEALING COMMENCES	25
FOCUS UPON INTEGRITY IN PLACE	27
BLESSINGS OF SAINT GERMAIN	29
ABOUT THE AUTHOR	39
LIGHT OF THE SOUL FOUNDATION	53

Trust and Betrayal
A Challenge of Choice

Saint Germain
06-12-2023

As Twin Flames, Soul Mates, and Ones in relationships of all types will likely observe, life-lessons persist, … inflowing in abundance even during significant physical separation periods, … lessons centered around Soul contracts. These challenging times present healing opportunities when mirrored wounds and vulnerabilities from being together have their chance to bubble up and be ripe for healing. Underpinning this healing process comes Trustworthiness, Honesty, and Respect which form a foundational nucleus *enabling agreements to be relied* upon, … further allowing co-operation, loyalty, accountability, harmony, and progress to thrive … in a win-win context.

<u>Among the top 'challenges of choice' on the list of the Human interactions ... inevitably comes the quandary raised by Trust and Betrayal.</u> Such opportunities for growth are intensified in Soul Mate and Twin Flame and All relationships, very often popping up near the top of the stack and giving impetus to periods of separation for healing.

<u>These enormous life-lesson incidents are paramount in all relationships and deeply imbedded in Divine healing dynamics, ... to be certain! Exactly how the Blessed gift of Human Free-will choice is chosen to be used ... exposes the very core of Trust and Betrayal Dynamics!</u>

To clarify, My dissertation of Wisdom today applies equally to *Soul Mates, Twin Flames and Others alike,... as* many of the evolutionary life-lessons are fundamentally the same, although of different intensities. Your Earth sources will clarify for you the distinction between *Soul Mates and Twin Flames,* a discussion nicely sorted out by certain of your Spiritual mediums in contact with Us Above.

Ones with clear intention, resolute about being of quality, *will in the end, ... find Mastering this process* to be one of the most enlightening, *purifying, rewarding Humankind.* as We pay great your healing

and self-available to **Introspection** proceed will dividends for and growth.

So, Carpi Diem Good People!
Unhealed, without Trust replacing Betrayal, a lingering layer of wounds can fester and destroy what otherwise could be healed in a victorious manner with persistent discipline, Wisdom, and Love. Such <u>unattended wounds,</u> as you may have noted by now, even with 1000 wonderful acts of reconciliation placed on top, can commonly prevail and remain unforgiven in the minds of Ones Betrayed.

This festering condition can effectively nullify copious acts of goodness lain on top if the wound itself remains unaddressed, unhealed. Moreover, this leaves a wound to be ongoingly endured, *especially for the offended One's Ego that experiences the betrayal,* **actual *or* simply in its own illusionary reality.**

You will need to remain focused as triggers of Betrayal are experienced, ... disconcerting, disturbing, and disorienting as they will no doubt be!

THE JOY OF BEING PRESENT

FOCUS ON YOUR *HEART*

STOP OVERTHINKING

LET GO OF YOUR DOUBTS FEARS ASSUMPTIONS,

AND

SURRENDER TO YOURSELF ABOUT "WHAT IS"

ENJOY THE PEACE!

Beyond a challenging 3-D scenario in the present day, there are *extended consequences*. Deferred potent life-lessons result in reoccurrences imbedded in future incarnations. *Fragmented Soul energies* needing corrective healing will remain so until brought into alignment, transformed from an unruly fragment, and purified for inclusion in the Soul body itself.

So be the sad outcome for *deferred life-lessons* until healing is in place. 3-D, Third Dimensional healings can surely be accomplished among awake Chelas, and then, more significant purification awaits, harboured within the 5th Dimension, *for those in that vibration.* Beyond the 5th Dimension, the healed lessons of Trust and Betrayal have already anchored themselves in Mastery by the Blessings of purification.

Also, bear in mind, and *not to minimize the betrayal* that may have *offended*, Both Twin Flames, Soul Mates and Other One's **perceptions of betrayal become all important.** It can be regarded as a growth and healing opportunity, or as the deal-breaker of the century! Ponder this!

A personal code of honor comes into play when earning and establishing Trust. When a Chela's *code of honor* is permanently imbedded, this *high standard* becomes a visceral way of Being, … a fundamental learning process and relationship building block elevated to gigantic importance.

In past centuries on Earth, a Handshake was offered and received as evidence that you were unarmed, and also as a contractual bonding of your agreement, … a mini ritual, … a promise, … which would then 'seal the deal', as you would say. And yes, handshakes can be gender-non- specific. (Master chuckles haaaa hmmmm).

I implore you to honor your handshake! Your Handshake, actual or figurative by your signature or verbal promise, … is a bond that seals a contract, an agreement pledged to be kept.

> *Let your agreements and promises be sacred unto to you, as a matter of unshakeable principle, ... a sacred promise from You to You!*

I will know if you break your promise, be certain. If so, I will take your ice cream away. (Master chuckles uuuuh uuuuh). Do you like your synchronicities?

P*rocessing breach of Trust incidents with healing as a primary objective ... as opposed to a lingering fixation upon making another* One *wrong ... and wrong forever without Forgiveness ... freshly brings in Love, possibility, and future happiness into the picture.*

Now that said, let's get down to the nitty gritty of all this! Open your hearts, be vulnerable to admitting what needs to be exposed about your behaviors, ... *right down to the bone,* ... and settle into the Truth that will clean and set things straight. Invoke a marvelous Process that will anchor your integrity within a special sacred space in your conscience <u>and</u> consciousness, now and

forever as long as you *honor* your vows and promises here!

If you are alert and awake, signs of behaviors that need your attention and correction will appear to you, perhaps best recognized by your own conscience resting within your *Highest-self*. And now, here come true *gifts of process,* delivered right in your lap.

The roots of betrayal center around broken promises, as in broken agreements. A broken agreement *will unfortunately,* ... to one degree or another ... violate and cross the other One's Boundary(s), if integrity be their code ... less there be double standards in play. (Master, hmmmmm).

Testing Boundaries. This is a favorite ploy of One intending to water down or not fully carry through on a promise. This covert tactic is employed to test the 'wiggle room' in an agreement already in place. Such <u>overtures to *Betrayal*</u> can lead to further consequences, and if allowed, the outcome becomes muddied, combined with the *fumes of Betrayal*. Have you ever tested the boundary(s) of your agreements?

Also, tangled with Betrayal is the behavior of lying, or even telling ½ Truths, to be clear. When you have lied, you have dishonored yourself as well as others involved. Lying is a step child of betrayal for sure. No doubt.

Recognize the *Truth* of your behaviors in this light and make the *needed self-corrections*, which only you may know about. Feeling that you may not be 'caught' is often an incentive to lie. Even if undetected, you yourself will know that this needs your attention and healing. Promise yourself! *Living with your own lies is a burden* that no Chela will want to tolerate.

At this point, you will serve yourself well to be alert to Boundaries, ... yours and others, which inevitably will come into the mix.

Alright!

T**rusting Ones** who are receiving your promise(s) understandably *rely on your integrity being included at the outset.* Wise Ones receiving promises will insure that *their understanding of a promise is crystal clear* when a promises is accepted. After that, if a promise is broken, Betrayal becomes a strong energy that takes

over, altering the quality and regard for *future interactions ... <u>sometimes with disbelief</u>!*

Skepticism and/or general disbelief of another's promises can arise *with Betrayal lingering about*, becoming very damaging to the cohesive glue that once beautifully held these very Twins together in honor, harmony and Trust.

At this point, **Forgiveness can start a healing process,** ... provided that new promise(s) are *made and kept with utmost integrity*. If this prevails, all can be well, and healing remains, sealed in place. I speak of promises to One's self as well as to others.

If Forgiveness not be present, B*etrayals* are sadly much more difficult to heal. People often recall ... " Burn me once shame on YOU, ... Burn me twice, shame on ME", and now possibilities for Trust go right out the window. Second chances with this reality in place are unfortunately at a premium among those *with Ego blockages and without Forgiveness* <u>spotlighted *in their hearts.*</u>

I heartily endorse putting the 'spotlight on Forgiveness' coupled with the Wisdom of healing! Open your Heart and let the Love shine in!

For a demonstration of this ... is win-win energy placed in action. Read My books, especially VICTORY FOR THE SOUL, *Relationships that Work*, Gordon Corwin II   Amazon   2022. This book goes hand in hand with TRUST AND BETRAYAL you are now reading.

As for Habitual **promise breakers,** *however slight*, they continue their own downslide, destroying their very foundation, within and without, often justifying their acts by excuses ... addictions of all sorts, uncontrollable urges, lies, physical challenges, mental lapses, and so on.

And at times, heartful acts and apologetic deeds of true virtue *by the promise breaker* are lovingly lain upon the situation in reconciliation, and then often met with rejection by a Twin who's 'Boundary' has been breached, as an incursion **yet to be forgiven.**

That is another conversation about **rising up to Forgive** and turn the other cheek. Many times easier said than done, I realize. A conversation for another day, Good Friends. Furthermore, at times, *even in the face of multiple virtuous deeds by the promise breaker* wanting to make up for the breach and correct it, ... reactivating recollections *by the One Betrayed,*   strongly overshadowing

these fine efforts to heal. Do you know where I AM going with this?

***Reactivation* of an incident**(s) in the eyes of the offended Soul Mate, Twin, or One who's Boundary has been crossed, … can further complicate and prolong the healing process. Reactivation recreates the incident(s) in a *present-time consciousness*, making it potent and very real again, as it was in the beginning!
Sometimes referred to as *holding a grudge.* And yes, ... still another conversation for another day.

Calculated Betrayals
Here is where the smart rats come out to deceive and manipulate, using their often covert and clever versions of Betrayal. Their motivation is that they 'think they are smart enough not to get caught'! Pure and simple. They have a high degree of confidence they 'will get away with it'. Their moves are often premeditated, refined and calculated to a high degree. They realize the risk, and are still willing to take it, often *overlooking the harshness of possible consequences.*

And, … there is a second part of this. If a calculating Betrayer does 'get away with it', there remains the karma and the stigma of guilt that can hang on, … far beyond the time frame of the

Betrayal. <u>Nagging thoughts about such an act *out of Divine Alignment will haunt those of conscience*</u>.

Repeat Betrayers, can be likened, in a mild way, to being *your own fallen Angel*, as a metaphor would have it. And remember, healing with <u>Truth and integrity in action</u> will reverse this dive, allow you to climb back up, *no longer be fallen*, and **reinstate your self-esteem within**, ...*and redraw your image in the eyes of others.*

Heal**ing will commence** when full disclosure and responsibility takes place, along with appropriate rectification(s) and true Forgiveness by All.

The healing is complete when *Forgiveness, Love and Surrender unto the Truth* <u>replace</u> the lingering emotions, reactivations, and damage of the breach. At this point, Twins and Ones are cleared and then can <u>choose to</u> <u>pledge moving forward in Trust,</u> as they may have been experiencing <u>before the Betrayal took place.</u>
This is a mini-process all of its own, as you can appreciate!

   Promise Revisions. Important to interject, ... here is a perfectly honorable action in context of promises made. If One is truly experiencing great

difficulty in keeping a promise, this can be sincerely and Truthfully shared with Another, a Twin, or a Soul Mate … and *thus openly explored together* for possible new ground to be uncovered as a *mutual agreement revision.*

An agreed upon Re-Promise, if you will. A Re-cast with mutual agreement!

<u>Herein is another opening for My famous win-win solution dynamics to enter the picture, wrapped in the open Truth of the matter, AND willingly accepted by all.</u>

O**N a bright side, time itself, with integrity now in place,** will open the door to heal Betrayal, building back the relationship on a solid foundation that *can be <u>relied upon.</u>* Confidence surely can be re-established, …
provided that integrity is meticulously kept in place, never allowing a <u>sliver of further doubt</u> to enter the behaviors of anyone involved. I admit, this is a tall order. And you are up to the task!

With integrity and sincerity firmly in place, the next step may be taken. Healing and *True* Forgiveness of Broken Trust combines here with Integrity and Compassion, ... to *meet the Challenge of Choice for All Ones involved in processing Trust and Betrayal life lessons.*

When Betrayal of Trust is experienced and then followed by sincere, honest, and true apology delivered by the promise Breaker, a healing opportunity opens up for the promise Holder to freely *choose to re-establish in good faith* the original Trust that was lost.

I Heartily endorse you to discover the Magic of True Unconditional Forgiveness without reservation.

Herein lies the *Challenge of Choice,* Dear Friends. Let your intuition, your Highest-self, and an open-Heart guide you.

    Once anchored as a visceral part of a whole Being, Integrity will prevail, front and center, in all interactions and in all self-talk thoughts alike! Remember, this uncompromising stand is visceral, a personal code of conduct with FULL integrity, … unalterable… and without exception or justification … to others or to self!

   This code may seem to an Ego like a horribly burdensome life-time noose around the neck, …

and yes, a cinch unescapable for some! Look around!

And yet, … <u>once *You* habitually *bathe yourself in the waters of Truth*</u>, just the opposite will enter your reality, and a new uplifting sense of joy Freedom will be your Blessing!

I wish for All a glorious outcome in patiently working through the challenging situations that are orchestrated by these special dynamics lain upon your tables. I assure you they are among the most potent energy lessons appearing in your Personal Universes.

Be heartened as you await results of the magnificent strides ahead in your Journeys of Upward Conscious Evolution through the Higher Dimensions ahead, My Dearest Ones.

With Our Fondest Blessings,

Saint Germain
And Lah Rahn Ananda aka
Gordon Corwin II

DISCLAIMER

The information contained within this Book is strictly for educational purposes. This Book and the Book's elements are provided to readers committed to Spiritual education, self-discovery, self-actualization, and transformation to align individual belief systems with a common source, Our Creator and Spirit, as the guiding light to enter doorways of change, new possibilities, growth, and manifestations within reach of an extraordinary and self-examined Human lifetime. Readers are encouraged to choose, of their own free- will and volition, to accept, to follow, or to reject the guidance, ideas, philosophies, stated truths, and techniques presented herein. If you wish to apply ideas and guidance contained herein, you are taking full responsibility for your actions. This Book contains information and general advice that is intended to help the readers to be better informed about physical, mental, emotional, and Spiritual well-being. Always consult your doctor for your individual needs. This Book is not intended to be a substitute for the medical advice of a licensed physician. The reader should consult with their doctor in any matters relating to his/her health. This Book contains information and general advice about business pursuits. This book is not intended to be a substitute for financial or legal advice. Reader is advised to consult your licensed financial or legal professional for such matters. In no event does the author or the publisher make guarantees, express or implied, as to results or consequences arising out of or related to the reader's use or inability to use the book's contents. Both the author and Highland Light Publishers (the publisher) do not assume and hereby disclaim any liability to any party for any loss, direct, indirect, or consequential damages, accidental, unintentional, or unforeseen, pain, suffering, emotional distress, or disruption resulting from the reader's negligence, actions or non-actions, accident, or any other cause.

About the Author

ordon Corwin II, also known as Lah Ran Ananda, translated literally as 'God Light Messenger', is a native Californian, educated at UC Berkeley, followed by service as a Commissioned US Naval Officer, and by extensive careers in the computer and real estate industries.

In 1995, Gordon clearly heard Lord Saint Germain's resounding and mysterious voice from Above, recruiting him to immediately engage with Ascended Spirit and follow his Soul's calling to reactivate his considerable past life Atlantean DNA channeling abilities, and to begin walking his Dharma to serve Humanity!

As an appointed Masters' Representative, Lah Rahn then began delivering Ascended energies through channeling of the Masters' words and visual media, which would now become his changed and conscious life path. In 1998 he founded The Light of the Soul Foundation, a qualified non-profit entity for advanced Spiritual education and Human philanthropy.

Following years of ego-cleansing by the Masters and his upward movement through Higher Dimensions of consciousness, Lah Rahn Ji has, for 25 years now, delivered clear and engaging channelings in public and private Spiritual events along with potent and enlightening mentoring of Chelas in The Light of the Soul Vortex in Southern California.

In 2007 he was highly honored to be chosen by Lord Saint Germain to be the Ascended Masters' instrument and Partner to begin, and later complete, this precise and accurate channeling to Earth of The Saint Germain Chronicles Collection, *A Journey Into Practical Spirituality 2008-2014*. In 2020 Lah Rahn again partnered with Saint Germain to author Victory for The Soul, *Relationships that Work*, pub 2022, and RISING ABOVE, *A Journey Into Higher Dimensions*, pub 2022, followed by TRUE COMPASSION, *Merging Love Into Oneness*, pub 2023, and now comes DUALITY, *In Perspective*, … all Titles found on Amazon, Gordon Corwin II. Other unpublished channel works include those from Ascended Masters Quan Yin and El Morya.

Lah Rahn aka Gordon Corwin currently lives in Oceanside, California and is available for private channelings and group events, and interviews as well as public speaking engagements.

Contact:

GordonCorwin24@gmail.com

Lah@SaintGermainChronicles.com

ACKNOWLEDGEMENTS

Once again, I Am overjoyed to acknowledge you who have contributed in so many different ways to this book, Truth and Betrayal, *A Challenge of Choice.*

You generous Ones have graciously given your love, time, and ongoing support to the success of writing and publishing this book, using unique creative talents and abilities, artistry, technical skills, financial resources, and much more.

Please know that YOU are most highly appreciated! Without your support, this book would not have been born as it is into life for all of those who would surround themselves with *A Challenge of Choice.*

My heartful thanks goes out to you all, with best wishes for your continued advancement along your Spiritual journey and in your varied careers of endeavor. I continue to send, along with Ascended Master Saint Germain, highest Blessings, admiration and love.

Lah Rahn Ananda
aka Gordon Corwin II

LLantar Chris Gulve, my longtime loyal friend and Spiritual Chela, for your inspiration and support to begin this *sixth* published book of channeled Wisdom dedicated to enlightening Human lives in those many vitally important facets of healing Betrayal with Truth, a practice that you hold near and dear to your heart. Your selfless and steady encouragement throughout the creation of this book, along with contributing most capable and diligent proof reading of the manuscript, has been of value beyond description. You are acknowledged with the greatest of appreciation, with many grateful thanks from both myself as the Author and Ascended Master Saint Germain and the Realm. Love and Blessings to you. Proof reading services from: llantar@sbcglobal.net

Jossue Legaspi Aguiere, my brother in this lifetime and Soul compadre over several past-lives, I salute you for your enthusiastic willingness to support the creation of my work with Spirit. Your consciousness and Soul have rapidly grown to be an *extraordinary messenger of life's lessons* dynamically delivered to the Author in real time during the channeling process of this book. You continue to gift quality experiences of value in friendship, comradery, and adventure, many of which were and are so very inspirational in creating this work for Humanity. You have my friendship, love and gratitude always.

Tim Yargeau, with special thanks for your kind and enthusiastic co-operation in applying your creative and very effective graphic design and photography skills, just when they were most needed! The results of your fine work, begun with the Saint Germain Chronicles Collection book project, greatly enhancing the true beauty of many graphic displays throughout the book as well. Your many image creations were also used in Saint Germain's new book 'VICTORY FOR THE SOUL, *Relationships that Work'* which has been written and is now published and available on Amazon.
t.yargeau@gmail.com

Teri Rider, for the spectacular graphic design and image creation of the Highland Light Monogram and LOGO, banner and all!
www.teririder.com

Elaine Johnson, my old friend from Junior High School in Highland, California. After many years, we have reconnected and are able to enjoy the past and now present times together. Many thanks for your willing and gracious support in the important proof reading process of publishing this new book! Many Blessings to you.

Marius Michael-George, for the most beautiful licensed, color images of your paintings, presenting likenesses of Ascended Masters Saint Germain and El Morya. Artwork © Marius Michael-George
www.Mariusfineart.com

Dreamstime.com, for your print licensed permission to utilize graphic images that add so much to illustrate text, solely inside the book in various places, with imagination and beauty.
Dreamstime.com

FCIT Florida Center for Instructional Technology, for the licensed use of your copyrighted, beautiful floral, ornate, and decorative capital letters to illustrate text, inside of the book.
licensing@fcit.us

123RF Limited, for your beautiful graphic images, print licensed for Our use, adding so much illustrative vitality in various places, solely inside of the book.
123RF.com

Public Domain, for location of the Comte Saint Germain portrait, and the circa 1864 Charles Sindelar public domain original portrait image of Saint Germain.
The Public Domain Review

The Light of the Soul Foundation is a Charitable non-profit 501 (c) (3) Philanthropic Organization founded in 1998 by Gordon Corwin, Trustee.

This non-denominational Foundation is dedicated to

The Spiritual Enlightenment of Humanity.

LOSF continues to be harmoniously bonded with

Highland Light Publishers,

sharing this Spiritual mission that includes writing, publishing and distributing Masters' books in addition to delivering live events with wisdom from The Ascended Masters Above.

"Bringing the Light of Spirit into the *every-day lives* and *consciousness* of the masses in an increasingly troubled earthly world … is the practical gift We lovingly offer".

As you now may observe, the collective behavior of Humanity

present dark and pervasive behaviors that prevail without change. Your kind philanthropy, donations, and bequests provide the financial means enabling Us to continue serving and delivering *Enlightenment from Above*, expanding Our outreach of Light. Your donations are transformed into the highest vibrations from Above to all Ones aspiring to reach and live their full Dharma's potential of heightened awareness, Love, Compassion and Soul evolvement … which awaits Humanity.

Light of the Soul Foundation

Charitable N**on-profit 501 (c) (3)**

Public Events and Spiritual Counseling

IRS **EIN: 91-1945098**

For Your Gifts, Donations, or Bequest Confirmations, By Check, Credit Card or Wire:

We are deeply grateful to Donors, Contributors and Philanthropists for your fine and generous *Gifts of Grace to uplift The Human Consciousness.*

You are an immensely essential resource that ongoingly empowers Our continuing Outreach.

For over two decades, We have delivered gifts of
Soul Enlightenment and Practical Spirituality via
recently published channeled works, along with
public events and
Spiritual readings ... with your generous support!

Many Thanks and Blessings. *You All* are Most Appreciated!

Gratefully yours, Gordon Corwin / Lah Rahn

Please Contact: Trustee, Gordon Corwin, Oceanside, CA 92056

Gordon@gordoncorwin.com   or

Gordoncorwin24@gmail.com

Light of the Soul Foundation

IRS   **EIN: 91-1945098**

Copyright 1998 – 2023. All rights reserved by Highland Light Publishers and Gordon W. Corwin II. Reproduction in any form, including foreign translations, radio broadcasts, video and YouTube content on any platform, movies, television shows, entertainment or informational programming, trailers, bonus material, scrips, code, images, artwork, all publications or storage, electronic or otherwise are our copyrighted property and may only be used with the express written permission of Highland Light Publishers and Gordon W. Corwin II; such permission will not be unreasonably withheld.

Contact Lah Rahn: Lah@saintgermainchronicles.com

Gordoncorwin24@gmail.com

NOTES

NOTES

NOTES

NOTES

www.ingramcontent.com/pod-product-compliance
Lightning Source LLC
Chambersburg PA
CBHW041400160426
42811CB00101B/1505